The Five Senses

Smelling

Rebecca Rissman

Heinemann Library
Chicago, Illinois

www.heinemannraintree.com
Visit our website to find out more information about Heinemann-Raintree books.

To order:
☎ Phone 888-454-2279
🖳 Visit www.heinemannraintree.com to browse our catalog and order online.

Edited by Rebecca Rissman and Catherine Veitch
Designed by Ryan Frieson and Kimberly R. Miracle
Original illustrations © Capstone Global Library
Illustrated by Tony Wilson (pp. 10, 12, 22, 23)
Picture research by Tracy Cummins
Originated by Heinemann Library
Printed in China by South China Printing Company Ltd

14 13 12 11 10
10 9 8 7 6 5 4 3 2 1

Library of Congress Cataloging-in-Publication Data
Smelling / Rebecca Rissman.
p. cm. -- (The five senses)
ISBN 978-1-4329-3681-5 (hc) -- ISBN 978-1-4329-3687-7 (pb)
QP458.R55 2010
612.8'6--dc22
2009022288

Acknowledgments
The author and publishers are grateful to the following for permission to reproduce copyright material: Corbis pp. **9** (© Tom Stewart), **17** (© moodboard), **18** (© Peter Turnley); Getty Images pp. **4** (Werner Dieterich), **6** (Burke/Triolo Productions), **7** (JJ), **11** (CO2), **13** (arabianEye), **14** (Johannes Rodach), **15** (Andreanna Seymore), **16** (VEER/Steve Cicero); PhotoEdit Inc. p. **19** (© David Young-Wolff); Photolibrary p. **20** (Jupiterimages); Shutterstock pp. **5** (© svitlana10), **8** (© Rafal Olechowski), **23 B** (© Rafal Olechowski), **23 C** (© svitlana10); Tom Pantages Photography p. **21** (© Tom Pantages).

Cover photograph of a boy smelling a flower reproduced with permission of Shutterstock (© zhuda). Back cover photograph of a girl smelling a flower reproduced with permission of Shutterstock (© Rafal Olechowski).

The publishers would like to thank Nancy Harris, Yael Biederman, and Matt Siegel for their assistance in the preparation of this book.

Every effort has been made to contact copyright holders of any material reproduced in this book. Any omissions will be rectified in subsequent printings if notice is given to the publisher.

Contents

Senses

We all have five senses.

We use our senses every day.

Smelling and seeing are senses.

Tasting, touching, and hearing are also senses.

How Do You Smell?

You use your nose to smell.

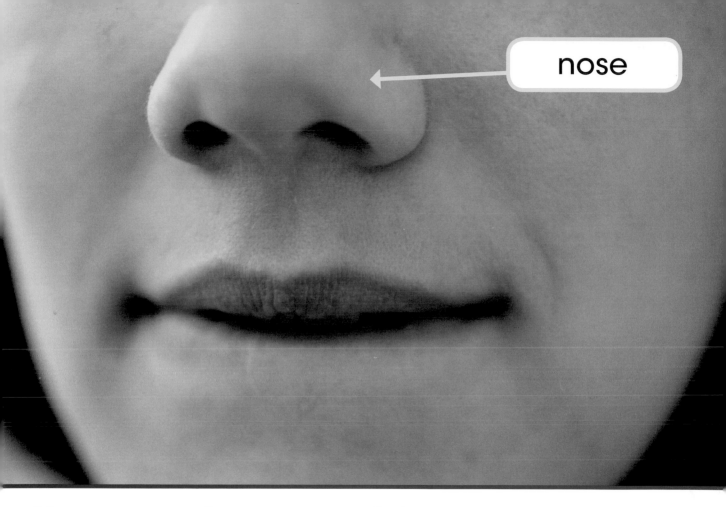

nose

Your nose is on your face.

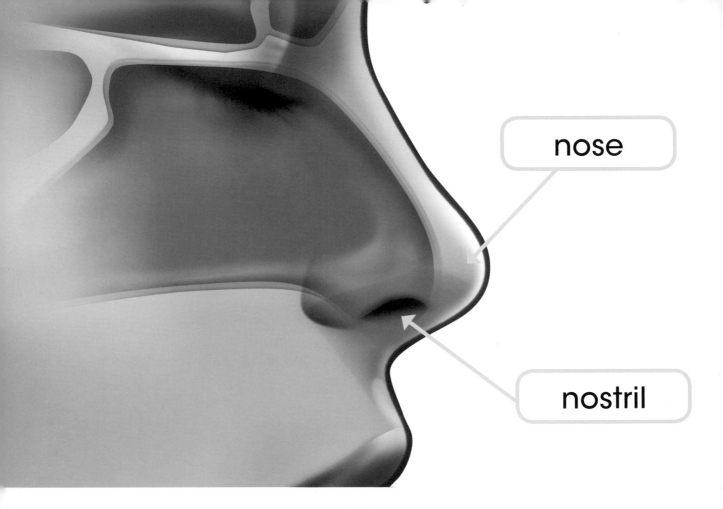

nose

nostril

You breathe air into your nose through nostrils.

Your nose smells things in the air.

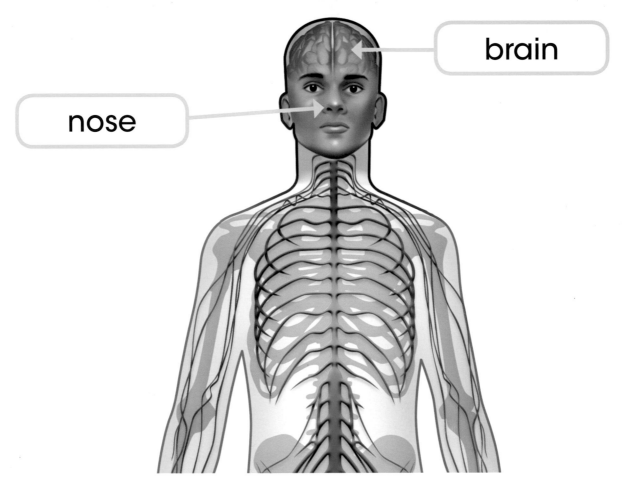

brain

nose

Your nose sends messages to your brain.

Your brain tells you what you
are smelling.

What Do You Smell?

You can smell plants.

You can smell animals.

You can smell food cooking.

You can smell flowers.

Smell Can Protect You

You can smell smoke.

You can smell things that are rotten.

Unsafe Smells

Some smells are bad for you.
Smelling some glues can make
you sick.

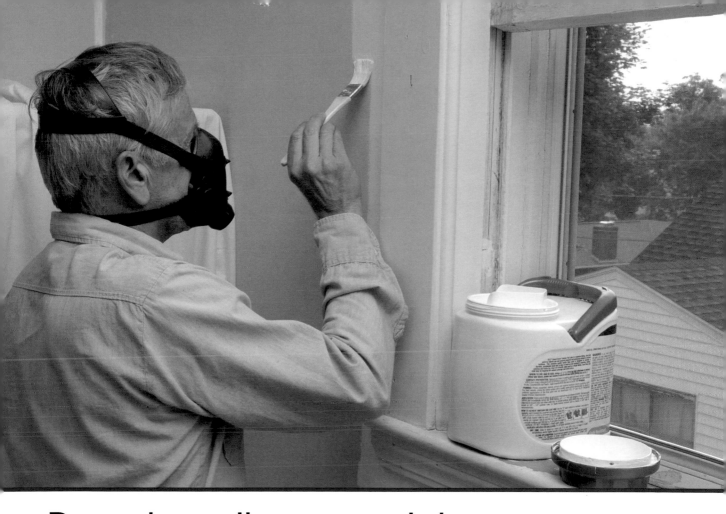

Do not smell some paints.
Smelling some paints can make
you sick.

Naming the Parts You Use to Smell

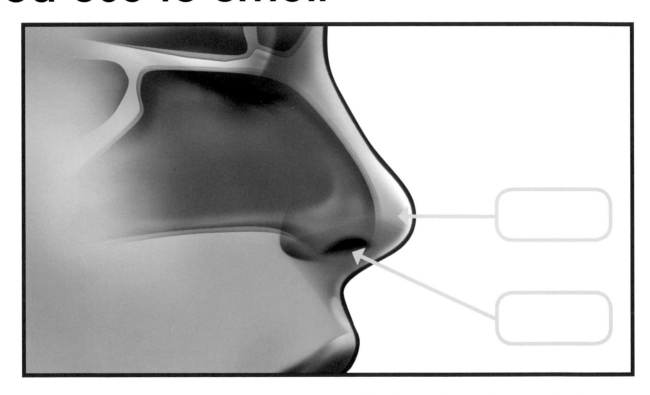

Point to where these labels should go.

nose   nostril

Answer on page 10.

Picture Glossary

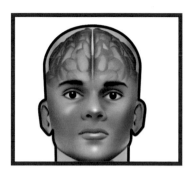

brain part of your body inside your head that helps you think, remember, feel, and move

nostril one of two holes in your nose where air goes in and out

sense something that helps you smell, see, touch, taste, and hear things around you

Index

Note to Parents and Teachers

Before reading

Explain to children that people use five senses to understand the world: seeing, hearing, tasting, touching, and smelling. Tell children that there are different body parts associated with each sense. Then ask children which body part they think they use to smell. Tell children that they use their nose to smell.

After reading

•Show children the diagram of the nose on page 22. Ask them to point to where the label "nostril" should go.

•Blindfold a child and give them a selection of things to smell. Can he or she guess what they are smelling?

•Make a list of smells that children like, and a list of smells they do not like. Ask children if they think bad smells act as a warning. Explain that some smells, such as smoke or rotten food warn them of danger.

24